Next Generation ENERGY

ENERGY FROM EARTH'S CORE

Geothermal Energy

James Bow

CRABTREE
Publishing Company
www.crabtreebooks.com

![Crabtree Publishing Company logo]

Crabtree Publishing Company

www.crabtreebooks.com

Author: James Bow

Editors: Sarah Eason, Jen Sanderson, and Shirley Duke

Proofreader: Katie Dicker and Wendy Scavuzzo

Editorial director: Kathy Middleton

Design: Paul Myerscough and Geoff Ward

Cover design: Paul Myerscough

Photo research: Sarah Eason and Jen Sanderson

Prepress technician: Margaret Amy Salter

Print coordinator: Margaret Amy Salter

Consultant: Richard Spilsbury, degree in Zoology, 30 years as an author and editor of educational science books

Written and produced for Crabtree Publishing by Calcium Creative

Library and Archives Canada Cataloguing in Publication

Bow, James, 1972-, author
       Energy from Earth's core : geothermal energy / James Bow.

(Next generation energy)
Includes index.
Issued in print and electronic formats.
ISBN 978-0-7787-1979-3 (bound).--
ISBN 978-0-7787-2002-7 (paperback).--
ISBN 978-1-4271-1637-6 (pdf).--
ISBN 978-1-4271-1629-1 (html)

       1. Geothermal resources--Juvenile literature. I. Title.

GB1199.5.B69 2015   j333.8'8   C2015-903212-1
                                            C2015-903213-X

Library of Congress Cataloging-in-Publication Data

Bow, James, author.
  Energy from Earth's core : geothermal energy / James Bow.
       pages cm. -- (Next generation energy)
  Includes index.
  ISBN 978-0-7787-1979-3 (reinforced library binding : alk. paper) --
ISBN 978-0-7787-2002-7 (pbk. : alk. paper) --
ISBN 978-1-4271-1637-6 (electronic pdf) --
ISBN 978-1-4271-1629-1 (electronic html)
1. Geothermal resources--Juvenile literature. 2. Power resources--Juvenile literature. 3. Geothermal engineering--Juvenile literature. 4. Clean energy industries--Juvenile literature. I. Title.

GB1199.5.B674 2016
333.8'8--dc23
                                      2015020967

Crabtree Publishing Company

www.crabtreebooks.com   1-800-387-7650

Printed in Canada/082015/BF20150630

Published in Canada
Crabtree Publishing
616 Welland Ave.
St. Catharines, Ontario
L2M 5V6

Published in the United States
Crabtree Publishing
PMB 59051
350 Fifth Avenue, 59th Floor
New York, New York 10118

Published in the United Kingdom
Crabtree Publishing
Maritime House
Basin Road North, Hove
BN41 1WR

Published in Australia
Crabtree Publishing
3 Charles Street
Coburg North
VIC, 3058

Contents

What Is Energy?

Energy is everywhere. Our bodies use energy to move around. People use energy to run computers and turn on lights. Energy is the ability to do work.

There are many different types of energy. Heat and light are forms of energy. **Mechanical energy** moves things using simple machines such as levers, ramps, and pulleys. **Chemical energy** is released when different substances react with each other. **Nuclear energy** comes from **atoms** as they are pushed together or pulled apart. Atoms are the smallest possible parts of an element. Stored energy is called **potential energy** and moving energy is called **kinetic energy**.

What Is Green Energy?

Energy cannot be created or lost, it can only be **transformed**, or changed. Once the energy is transformed, however, it can be hard to change back. For example, if a piece of wood is burned, heat and light are given off, and ash, smoke, and **carbon dioxide** are produced. You cannot remake the wood once it is burned. When energy sources such as wood run out, they are called **nonrenewable**. Energy sources that are not so easily used up are called **renewable**.

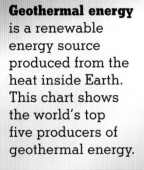

Geothermal energy is a renewable energy source produced from the heat inside Earth. This chart shows the world's top five producers of geothermal energy.

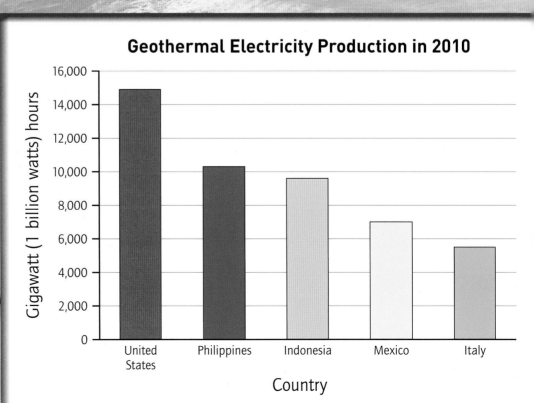

Geothermal Electricity Production in 2010

Gigawatt (1 billion watts) hours

| | United States | Philippines | Indonesia | Mexico | Italy |

Country

The ideal form of energy is one that gives power for as long as it is needed. It should also give off as little **pollution** as possible. Pollution is substances such as carbon dioxide, smoke, and ash that make land, water, or air dirty and unsafe. Energy that can give a lot of power with little pollution is good for the **environment**. It is called "green" energy.

On Earth, there are two main sources of energy: the energy reaching Earth's surface from the Sun, and the energy beneath Earth's surface. In this book, we will talk about how to harness the energy below Earth's surface—geothermal energy.

By using green energy such as geothermal power, the planet will be protected from dangerously high levels of pollution.

REWIND

People have been using geothermal power in the form of springs heated by Earth since the dawn of history. The oldest recorded hot spring spa was a stone pool built on China's Lisan Mountain in the 200s BCE. The Romans used hot springs for a number of their public baths. What benefits did this hot water provide for the Chinese and the Romans?

What Is Geothermal Energy?

The Sun hits Earth with 174 petawatts of energy. This is enough energy to power trillions of 100-watt light bulbs. Despite this, the Sun's energy does not reach more than 33 feet (10 m) below Earth's surface. Below that, the heat that is found comes from Earth itself.

When there is snow on the ground, it can be hard to imagine the enormous heat below Earth's surface. However, we can see the heat from inside Earth **erupting**, or exploding, as **lava** from volcanoes. Earth is a sphere 7,918 miles (12,743 km) in **diameter**. Of that, Earth's crust makes up just the top 43 miles (69 km). The rest of the planet is made up of the mantle and its core, both of which are hot enough to melt rock.

crust

upper mantle

mantle

outer core

inner core

Beneath Earth's crust are four different layers. It gets hotter and hotter near the outer and inner core.

Why Is Earth So Hot?

One of the reasons for the core's high temperatures is that, except for the crust, the planet still has not cooled down from when it formed 4.5 billion years ago. The **friction** that comes from **denser** materials sinking to Earth's center helps warm the planet, too. The third reason for Earth's high temperatures is radioactive decay. This occurs when atoms break down and lose parts of themselves, changing into different atoms, and releasing heat and light. These three factors make Earth's core reach 10,832°F (6,000°C). Scientists estimate that Earth's heat can provide 44.2 **terawatts** of power per year. A terawatt is 1 trillion watts—enough power to light up 10 billion 100-watt light bulbs and more than double the world's current energy needs.

Around the world, hot springs can be found where water warmed by volcanic heat rises to Earth's surface.

REWIND

The world's oldest district heating system is found in Chaudes-Aigues, France. The name of the town means "hot waters" in French. The town has 30 hot springs, the hottest of which is 180°F (82°C). Since the 1500s, the townspeople have used the 118,877 gallons (450,000 l) of hot water that flows from the springs each day to heat their homes. Only 1,000 people live in Chaudes-Aigues. The springs provide them with enough hot water, but how might the system need to change if more people move to the town?

Geothermal Energy Is Hot!

The sources for geothermal energy are most obvious near volcanoes. Anything that can heat rock to the point where it melts can provide a lot of energy. Even in places where volcanoes are dormant or extinct, the hot **magma** that created those volcanoes is still near the surface. Geothermal energy is plentiful in such places as well, and can be seen in a variety of ways.

Volcanoes are found mostly around the edges of **tectonic** plates. Tectonic plates are pieces of Earth's crust that float on the mantle.

The temperature of Earth 328 feet (100 m) below the surface is roughly 55°F (13°C). However, in areas where volcanoes exist or used to exist, magma chambers bring Earth's heat closer to the surface. Near the surface, the heat meets water that has seeped below the surface. The pressure of the rocks around the water keeps the water from boiling into steam, allowing it to reach temperatures of more that 212°F (100°C) and stay liquid. When that water comes to the surface and is released from the pressure of the rocks, it can burst into steam. Hot springs, **geysers**, and **fumaroles** are obvious signs of geothermal energy.

Energy for the Taking

In 1787, James Watt built the world's first steam engine. He used boiling water to turn a wheel. From this great steam engine came machines, automobiles, trains, and **generators** that changed the world. However, it can take a large amount of fuel to produce the energy needed to power machines and vehicles. Geothermal energy is efficient because there is no need to boil water. The energy can be used to heat homes, turn turbines to produce electricity, and much more.

Boise, Idaho, is close to the Rocky Mountains and near volcanic activity that provides geothermal heat.

REWIND

In 1892, the first geothermal-powered heating system in the United States was set up in Boise, Idaho. Today, this system still works, heating more than 65 businesses in Boise's downtown area. By 2010, there were 20 district heating systems throughout the United States. The systems are all in states with mountains and geothermal activity and they all each serve fewer than 300 customers. With this in mind, how useful can geothermal energy be to places far from hot springs and volcanoes?

Geothermal Energy Is Cool!

The temperature on Earth's surface changes all the time. But below the surface, the temperature is stable. At 25 miles (40 km) beneath the surface, the temperature is a constant 932°F (500°C). At 328 feet (99 m) beneath the surface, it is 55°F (13°C). As a result of this stability in temperature, even at that depth, Earth can provide us with energy needed to heat and cool our homes.

The Power of Stability

Today, holes 328 feet (100 m) deep are being drilled into Earth's surface. This drilling taps into a layer that is cooler than the surrounding air in summer and warmer than the surrounding air in winter. Water or air pushed through pipes laid through this layer can be heated or cooled to the temperature of the surrounding rock, before being brought back to the surface.

The warmer temperature on the ocean floor means that oceans freeze from the top to the bottom. This is why ice can be seen floating on the surface.

A similar system can be used in Earth's oceans and deepest lakes. As much as 98 percent of the Sun's energy is absorbed by the top 7 feet (2 m) of a body of water. While **currents** can move that warm water around, cooler, denser water usually settles on the bottom, where the Sun's energy cannot reach it. Unlike most liquids that become denser and heavier as they freeze, water reaches its greatest **density** at 39°F (4°C). This means that there is a steady supply of water at that temperature at the bottom of the oceans and many lakes, regardless of the season. This water can be used for cooling.

Fish, such as pike, live in many lakes. Geothermal energy developers must take care not to harm the wildlife while using the energy resources of lakes.

The Energy Future: You Choose

While geothermal energy is a renewable resource that produces few **greenhouse gases**, it is not without its problems. Pumping water underground to capture Earth's heat can pollute **groundwater**. If too much water is pumped through a system, the temperature of the surrounding earth can be changed. The temperature at the bottom of a lake can also rise. This can make a geothermal energy source less useful, and its heat pollution could harm a lake's **ecosystem**. Are these risks worth the energy that geothermal power provides? How do these risks compare to the risks of using oil and natural gas? Is there a chance technology might address some of these problems? In what way?

How We Harvest the Power

When it is plentiful, geothermal energy is easy to use. Constructing a building around a hot spring provides that building with warm water. For centuries, resorts have been built around hot springs. People take advantage of the hot water and many believe that the minerals **dissolved** in that water have health benefits.

Going Beyond Passive Heating

If people want to use geothermal energy beyond hot springs, they need machines that can harvest the springs' energy and make it useful. These machines can include turbines and **heat exchangers**. Turbines are generators that create electricity when they are turned by a mechanical force. Water that turns into steam can produce the pressure required to turn turbines.

Hot springs in Japan allow Japanese macaque monkeys to keep warm in areas where it snows for most of the year.

If there is no water to turn into steam, heat exchangers can be used to get the heat from the ground. These machines pump surface water to below the surface, where it is hot. They keep the water down there for some time, so it can absorb or take in heat from the surrounding rocks. The warm water is then brought back to the surface. If the rocks below the surface are cool, warm water at the surface can be cooled in the same way.

Using Geothermal Energy

Geothermal energy can also be used in **desalination**—removing salt from water. When water boils, the steam that rises has none of the salts or minerals found in water. When the steam condenses back into liquid, it becomes pure fresh water. Geothermal heat boils salty water without using fuel to provide the heat. **Aquaculture**, which is fish farming, also benefits from hot springs. Californian fish farmers use spring water to keep their ponds at the right temperature.

Piping hot water and steam from the source to where they will be used can require steam tunnels like this one in Denmark. As long as the water is under pressure at the source, additional pumping is not needed.

FAST FORWARD

In 2012, an Oregon company injected cold water at high pressure into hot rock 0.3 miles (0.5 km) below the surface in a process known as **fracking**. High-pressure cold water was pumped into the hot rocks underground. The company also pumped tiny bits of plastic into the cracks formed by the water to stabilize the cracks and keep them open. If this technique is proven safe, it could stop further cracking and make geothermal power available in more places. Fracking for oil exploration has been thought to cause some documented earthquakes. Is the benefit of more energy worth the risk?

Pros and Cons

No source of energy is perfect. They all have their own advantages and challenges. For example, solar power needs sunshine for it to work effectively, so it will not work very well in overcast conditions or at night.

One advantage geothermal energy has over most other green energy sources is that Earth supplies a steady temperature that can be used. As much energy as is needed, whenever it is needed, can be generated no matter what the weather conditions are or whether it is day or night. Energy such as this is described as "dispatchable." It is also easy to make use of geothermal energy. Apart from the energy required to pump water, little or no fuel is needed to use geothermal energy.

More Than Just Hot Water

Geothermal energy has its problems, however. If the steam is unavailable at the surface, it costs a lot of time and money to dig wells deep enough to reach it. The steam from geothermal wells often includes more than water because hot water dissolves minerals. These can include poisonous gases such as **hydrogen sulfide** and toxic elements such as **boron** and lead. Salts in the water can rust pipes and pollute streams. Calcium buildups can block pipes and cause leaks.

The brilliant colors of this hot spring in New Zealand are the result of **bacteria**, which feed on certain minerals in the springs at very high temperatures. Different bacteria survive at different temperatures and produce a range of colors.

Water is sometimes injected underground to heat it. Like fracking in oil and gas exploration, the pressurized water can possibly cause small earthquakes and pollute groundwater supplies.

Geothermal energy has a lot to offer as a stable and inexpensive energy source compared with other renewable sources. However, people need to understand the risks of using geothermal energy and prevent problems before they occur.

REWIND

Nevada had two large geyser fields, Steamboat Springs and Beowawe, until the 1980s. Then, the state began drilling to set up geothermal power plants at both locations. Both plants generated electricity with little air pollution and no greenhouse gas emissions. However, the plants pulled too much heated water from the ground and lowered the **water table**. As a result, the geysers on these two fields stopped working and no longer exist. Should Nevada have looked for a way to use the geothermal energy that did not harm these geysers? Was the loss of these geysers worth the production of pollution-free power?

Although it is expensive to set up a geothermal power plant, once this is done, the energy source is far cheaper than wind and solar power.

Geothermal Energy Under the Sea

With 70 percent of Earth covered by oceans, many of the world's geothermal sources are underwater. The oceans cover more than 40,000 miles (64,374 km) of mid-ocean ridges. There, tectonic plates pull apart and new crust is built up by magma that rises from Earth's mantle through volcanoes. Tapping these sources offers a number of advantages.

A Complex Ecosystem

Earth's crust beneath the oceans is thinner than the crust beneath land surfaces, making the oceans much closer to the heat of Earth's mantle. In most places on land, people must drill 1.7 miles (2.7 km) before the surrounding rock is hot enough to boil water. **Hydrothermal vents**, which are geysers found on the ocean floor near active volcanoes, spew out water at temperatures as high as 752°F (400°C).

Incredibly hot water can be seen spewing from hydrothermal vents along Earth's ocean floor.

However, many of these hydrothermal vents are buzzing with life seen nowhere else on Earth. Developing the geothermal sources could harm those creatures. The vents also pour out a lot of minerals and chemicals that have dissolved in the hot water. They can damage pipes and make collecting the hot water a challenge. Another problem is reaching the underwater vents, which can be more than 1.6 miles (2.6 km) beneath the ocean's surface.

Meeting the Challenge

Despite these challenges, using geothermal energy from hydrothermal vents beneath the ocean is being considered for sites in the Gulf of California in Mexico. Other countries that could try something similar include New Zealand and the Philippines.

Geothermal energy can power light bulbs! However, getting the power to the bulbs can be expensive and can disrupt the environment.

REWIND

Generating electricity from hydrothermal vents is just an idea at this point, but at one time, so was generating electricity from geothermal power. Italy's Prince Piero Ginori Conti tested the first geothermal power generator in 1904 at the Larderello dry steam field in Italy. He lit four light bulbs. The first commercial geothermal power plant started operating at Larderello in 1914. This was the world's only geothermal power plant until one was built in New Zealand in 1958. Why do you think it took people so long to further explore using geothermal energy for electric power?

The Geothermal Country

Iceland is an island country in the middle of the Atlantic Ocean, located between Great Britain, Greenland, and North America. Though it has a population of just 323,000 people, it is the world's largest producer of electricity per person. Around 25 percent of this power comes from geothermal sources.

Sitting on a Volcanic Battery

Iceland sits on top of the Mid-Atlantic Ridge, where the tectonic plates beneath the Atlantic Ocean are breaking apart and new crust is being formed as magma rises from the mantle. The island has hundreds of volcanoes, and at least 30 are active. All of that heat close to the surface means that there is a lot of geothermal activity in the form of geysers and hot springs. In fact, the word "geyser" comes from Iceland's Geysir, which still erupts and sends boiling water up to 230 feet (70 m) in the air.

Although Iceland's landscape is very beautiful, living near its volcanoes is risky. Throughout history, volcanic eruptions have killed thousands of people.

Realizing they had a huge amount of natural power for such a small country, the people of Iceland decided to generate most of their electricity through clean energy sources. Currently, hot water from geothermal wells heats 89 percent of the houses in Iceland. Along with **hydroelectric** and solar power, nearly all of Iceland's electricity is produced from renewable sources.

No More Fossil Fuels?

If Iceland can figure out how to use its renewable energy sources to power its automobiles, trucks, and boats, it could stop using **fossil fuels** such as coal, oil, and natural gas entirely. It would become the first country in the world to be "carbon neutral." Carbon neutral means that no carbon dioxide is emitted into the **atmosphere**, so the country does not contribute to global climate change. In Iceland, geothermal power is a **profitable**, or money-making industry, and many private companies are researching geothermal technology.

The Puhagen geothermal plant in the Philippines generates electricity for the country. It has 37 volcanoes, of which 18 are still active.

FAST FORWARD

The Philippines produces more geothermal energy than Iceland—1,904 **megawatts** (MW) compared to 575 MW—but that energy covers just 27 percent of its total needs. El Salvador gets 25 percent of its energy needs from geothermal sources. Look at maps of these two countries. What do they have in common with Iceland that makes it possible for them to get so much energy from geothermal sources?

The Power of the Geysers

The United States generates just 0.3 percent of its energy from geothermal sources. However, due to its size and population, it leads the world in geothermal power production at 3,086 MW.

There is a large potential source of geothermal power in the United States: Yellowstone National Park. Yellowstone is a large dormant volcano in Wyoming that has 500 geysers. Each year, thousands of tourists come to see a huge geyser named Old Faithful erupt. It sends as many as 8,454 gallons (32,000 l) of boiling water as high as 164 feet (50 m).

Beyond Yellowstone

Most geothermal energy in the United States is generated north of San Francisco. "The Geysers" is a 45-square mile (117 sq km) geothermal field. It produces up to 1,517 MW of power from 18 geothermal power plants and more than 300 wells drilled into the hot rocks. People have visited the area's hot springs for more than 12,000 years, beginning with Native Americans who used the water for bathing and cooking. In 1848, European-American settlers set up a resort there for tourists.

Throughout most of the United States, at 11 feet (3.3 m) below the surface, the temperature ranges from 167–347°F (75–175°C). The magma chamber lying beneath Yellowstone raises that temperature to more than 527°F (275°C).

In 1921, the first geothermal wells were drilled into the hot rocks beneath The Geysers. In 1960, the Pacific Gas and Electric company built a power plant there that could produce 11 MW of energy. By 1980, the area was mostly used by power plants and the original spa was abandoned. The amount of power taken from The Geysers has begun to use up the steam field. Power companies have dealt with this by injecting treated water from sewage plants deep underground. Not only has this allowed The Geysers to produce more geothermal power, but it has also diverted waste water that would have instead flowed into lakes and streams.

Yellowstone National Park is a home to thousands of **endangered animals**, including wolves and buffalo. Endangered animals are at risk of **extinction**, or dying out.

The Energy Future: You Choose

The energy produced by geothermal power plants is renewable and free of greenhouse gases. However, the power plants found in The Geysers are large and they disrupt the natural setting. Can the geothermal power of Yellowstone National Park be harvested without disrupting the local environment? Would it be better to leave Yellowstone alone and rely on other forms of energy? Support your answers with examples from your reading and research.

Keeping It Cool in Toronto

Toronto in Canada is a city on the shores of Lake Ontario. Since 2003, the Enwave Energy Corporation has drawn water through pipes reaching 3 miles (5 km) into that lake at a depth of 272 feet (83 m) below the surface. There, the water temperature stays at a steady 39°F (4°C) throughout the year. Using this water, Enwave cools dozens of skyscrapers throughout downtown Toronto.

Power Saver

While it costs a lot of money to lay pipes and power the pumps to move the water, Enwave's system saves the equivalent of 85 MW of power, which would otherwise be spent on air conditioners. Enwave has also designed the system to deal with concerns about heat pollution. After running through heat exchangers, the pumped water is added to Toronto's water supply instead of being returned directly to the lake.

The city of Halifax, Nova Scotia, has a district cooling system. It uses cold water from the bottom of its harbor to cool 699,654 square feet (65,000 sq m) of office space.

At the time, Toronto's district cooling system was the largest in the world, but other cities have started similar systems. Stockholm in Sweden uses a district cooling system in which cold water from the Baltic Sea is pumped through 127 miles (204 km) of pipes to cool more than 600 buildings, including universities, offices, and hospitals. Other systems include Cornell University in Ithaca, New York, which uses water from Cayuga Lake to cool its campus. In 2006, Amsterdam in Netherlands launched a system for a newly developed business district, taking in water from Lake Nieuwe Meer, saving 9.6 MW of air conditioning power.

The Pacific Ring of Fire is where the Pacific tectonic plate meets surrounding plates. It is home to 75 percent of the world's active and dormant volcanoes.

FAST FORWARD

The Ring of Fire describes the volcanoes that line the Pacific coasts of North and South America, as well as east Asia, including countries such as the United States, Mexico, and Japan. Canada is the only major country on the Pacific Ring of Fire that has not yet developed geothermal power. Geothermal fields in British Columbia and the Yukon are estimated to have enough energy to produce anywhere between 1,550 to 5,000 MW of electricity. What might be holding Canada back from developing its geothermal resources? Do you believe people are concerned about the use of technology to develop geothermal power?

Geothermal Limits

Geothermal energy can provide a long-lasting and stable supply of energy, but it can be hard to get that energy to the places that need it. Most geothermal energy sources have to be located near volcanic areas. For example, Yellowstone National Park has a lot of geothermal power, but no big cities nearby that could use the power.

Geothermal cooling systems can cool things at less cost and with fewer greenhouse gas emissions than the electricity required to run air conditioners. However, holes must be drilled and pipes laid to exchange the heat, which is something an average homeowner cannot afford to do.

Geothermal drilling can be costly and disruptive, but it can save on heating and air conditioning costs in the long run.

Thermal Efficiency

Another problem is geothermal energy's low thermal efficiency. Thermal efficiency describes how much energy is transformed into useful work. Light bulbs turn electricity into light, but also into heat. The old **incandescent** light bulbs that people had in their homes were hot to touch because they had a low thermal efficiency, wasting much of their power as heat. Compact fluorescent light bulbs (CFLs) and LEDs are cooler to touch because they generate light more efficiently.

The environmental effects of harvesting geothermal energy must be measured against the effects of mining and of burning fossil fuels.

Power plants that run on fossil fuels have a higher thermal efficiency. These plants boil water for steam, so they can heat water to higher temperatures than geothermal electric plants can reach. A large amount of fossil fuels is needed to reach these temperatures, but more power is produced than at geothermal plants. Many geothermal plants would be needed to supply the power provided by a few fossil-fuel-powered plants.

FAST FORWARD

Finding sources of geothermal energy requires some of the same techniques and methods used to find fossil fuels. Geothermal explorers use ground radar and explosions to build a picture of the ground below. Test wells are drilled to see how much water and heat are available. Some equipment even measures the changes in gravity and magnetic fields. The cost of exploring for geothermal energy can be as high as 42 percent of the cost of producing energy from geothermal sources. Given thermal efficiency, how might searching for geothermal sources compare to searching for fossil fuel sources? What part does technology play in the exploration and drilling?

The Challenges Ahead

Geothermal energy is very good at providing a stable source of energy that is inexpensive to use. However, like other green energy sources, there are challenges that have to be met before geothermal energy can replace fossil fuel use.

The United States alone used around 137 billion gallons (519 billion liters) of gasoline in 2014. Electrically powered vehicles exist and could be powered by electricity created by geothermal power. However, electric cars are not yet flexible enough to move far from their source of power. Therefore, using geothermal energy to power cars is currently not possible.

Portable Fuels

Developers in Iceland are considering using batteries to store the power generated by geothermal plants and cars could run on these batteries. However, they are expensive to make and difficult to recycle. Batteries also do not recharge as quickly as it takes to refuel a vehicle with gasoline.

Batteries can store electricity for later use, but they may lose 8–20 percent of their electrical charge each year.

Another solution could be to produce hydrogen gas. This is done by running electricity through water, breaking the **molecules** into hydrogen and oxygen atoms. The hydrogen gas can be burned like gasoline or can provide power to a portable electric generator, called a fuel cell. Iceland has developed the first hydrogen fueling stations that are to be used just like gas filling stations. However, there is still a problem of how to fit enough hydrogen into the gas tank of a vehicle, since hydrogen takes up far more space than gasoline. The technology is improving and, if successful, hydrogen fuel cells can also be used to bottle other green energy sources such as solar and wind power to fuel vehicles.

The most plentiful source for hydrogen gas is water, but taking water from the oceans will upset the balance of this ecosystem.

FAST FORWARD

Iceland has more geothermal energy than it needs. To sell that energy to Europe, it is hoping to build the longest undersea power cable in the world to connect to the continent's grid. There are concerns about this project, however. Power leaks could kill marine life. The magnetic fields around power lines could disrupt the biological electrical fields animals such as sharks and whales use to spot prey, find mates, or avoid predators. How could the consequences of these power lines affect the advantages of geothermal energy over other energy sources? How could the ecosystem be upset if whales or sharks lost use of their electrical sensing mechanisms?

Power Up!

Geothermal energy offers a lot of promise as a stable, renewable energy source, but there are challenges to overcome in using it. However, the same is true with all energy sources, including other green energy sources such as solar and wind. Perhaps the solution is to adopt a variety of energy sources and use less energy.

What Can You Do?

Walking and taking public transportation more, turning off lights when they are not being used, and buying energy-efficient light bulbs and appliances, means that fewer fossil fuels are used. It also makes it easier for greener alternatives to replace them. No one action or technology will save the world, but we can all make small steps toward it—and the first step begins with you!

By the time they become adults, today's students will see big changes to the ways energy is harvested and used.

To model a geothermal power plant using steam, try this experiment.

You Will Need:

- A hammer
- A small nail
- An empty tin can with one end cut off
- A ruler
- A small kitchen pot
- Water
- Aluminum foil
- Tape
- A stove
- An oven mitt
- A child's pinwheel
- Adult supervision

Instructions

1. Using the hammer and the nail, carefully punch two small holes in the bottom of the can, about 1 inch (2.5 cm) apart.
2. Fill the pot halfway with water and cover the top of the pot with aluminum foil. Pinch the foil around the edges to seal it.
3. Punch a small hole in the top of the foil cover.
4. Ask an adult to help you put the pot on the stove and bring it to a boil.
5. Once steam starts coming out of the hole in the foil, put on an oven mitt and hold the pinwheel over that hole. Note how fast the pinwheel spins.
6. Still wearing the oven mitt, place the can on top of the foil, open-end facing down, so the hole in the foil is in the center of the open end of the can.
7. When steam starts coming out through the two holes in the can, hold the pinwheel over the steam. Note how fast the pinwheel spins.
8. Turn off the stove and let the water cool. Poke more holes in the foil covering the pot.
9. Boil the water again. Hold the pinwheel over the original hole in the foil. How fast does the pinwheel turn now?

Steps 6 and 7

- pinwheel
- holes
- can
- foil
- pan

What Happened?

The tin can represents a geothermal power plant, and the pinwheel represents a turbine producing electricity. Each hole punched into the foil represents a geothermal well drilled to get at the steam. How does adding holes affect the amount of power available to the pinwheel? What happens when the water is low?

Glossary

Please note: Some bold-faced words are defined where they appear in the text

aquaculture The growing of fish in controlled ponds

atmosphere The layer of gases that surround Earth

bacteria Single-celled organisms that can be helpful and sometimes harmful

boron A shiny, nonmetallic element that comes mainly from borax

carbon dioxide A gas molecule made up of a carbon atom joined with two oxygen atoms

currents The flow of ocean and other bodies of water in a specific direction

denser More crowded or massed together for each unit of space

density A measurement showing how tightly packed and heavy something is

diameter A straight line passing from side to side through the center of a circle or sphere

dissolved Absorbed into water

ecosystem The plants, animals, and other organisms that live together in a specific environment

environment The conditions of the area where something lives

fossil fuels Energy sources made from the remains of plants and animals that died millions of years ago and were buried

fracking Injecting water or other liquids underground at high pressure

friction The resistance to movement that occurs when two objects are in contact

fumaroles Geothermal features where heat within Earth boils water that comes to the surface; Fumaroles release steam, not water.

generators Machines that change motion into electrical energy

geysers Natural hotsprings that can sometimes erupt with water or steam

greenhouse gases Gases in the atmosphere that contribute to the greenhouse effect

groundwater Water that is found underground

heat exchangers Machines that are used to transfer heat from one source to another

hydroelectric Electricity generated using the flow of water

hydrogen sulfide A colorless, poisonous gas; Its molecules are made up of one hydrogen atom and one sulfur atom.

incandescent Something that lights up when heated

lava Molten rock that flows from a volcano or from a crack in Earth's surface

magma Molten material below Earth's crust that comes out of volcanoes as lava and cools to form rock

megawatts Units of measure for energy; There are 1 million watts in a megawatt.

molecules Two or more atoms that have joined in a bond

petawatts Units of measure for energy. There are 1 quadrillion watts, or 1,000 gigawatts, in a petawatt

pollution Materials introduced into the environment and cause harmful or poisonous effects

tectonic The way Earth's crust is broken up into plates floating over Earth's mantle

terawatts Unit of measure for energy; There are 1 trillion watts in a terawatt.

water table The level of water under the ground

Learning More

Find out more about alternative energy and global climate change.

Books

Doeden, Matt. *Finding Out About Geothermal Energy*. Minneapolis, MN: Lerner Group, 2015.

Owen, Ruth. *Energy From Inside Our Planet: Geothermal Power* (Power: Yesterday, Today, Tomorrow). New York, NY: PowerKids Press, 2013.

Wachtel, Alan. *Geothermal Energy* (Energy Today). New York, NY: Chelsea Clubhouse, 2010.

Websites

Learn about the environment, play games, and do eco-related activities at:
www.ecokids.ca

Read about energy, how it is made, and how to stay safe around electricity at:
www.alliantenergykids.com

This site by the U.S. Energy Information Administration explains all about geothermal energy:
www.eia.gov/kids/energy.cfm?page=geothermal_home-basics

Find out more about global climate change, including discussions about alternative energy sources such as geothermal at:
www.epa.gov/climatestudents/index.html

Index